My Faraway Home

Written by Matilda May

Flying Start
to Literacy®

Contents

Introduction

Many people around the world live in towns and cities where there are lots of other people. Most of the things that they need are close by – shops, schools and hospitals.

But some people live in places that are a long way from towns and cities.

Living in these places can be difficult because there are no schools, hospitals or shops close by. But people who live in these places have ways of getting the things that they need.

Chapter 1:
My cattle station home

My name is Gus.
I live on a cattle station
in Australia.

Our cattle station is a long
way from everything,
including school.

This cattle
station
in Western
Australia
is the size of
a small country.

I cannot go to school
with other children because it would
take two days to get there. I have lessons
at home instead. I talk to my teacher using
a computer and the Internet.

I also get to talk to other kids who do
lessons at home like I do.

I get activities and home lessons delivered by a plane, which visits our cattle station once a week with food and other supplies.

My teacher visits me by plane three times each year to talk to me about my learning.

Every year, I go to
town for a school camp.
I travel for two days to get to town.
I get to see the other kids in my class.
We play games, have swimming lessons
and learn team sports.

Chapter 2:
My canyon home

My name is Carla. I live in a village at the bottom of the Grand Canyon, in the USA.

There is no road into our village, but there is a steep track.

This village, Supai, is inside the Grand Canyon.
It is a Native American village.

Everything we need is delivered by mules, which are a type of horse. They walk along the steep track. The mules are tied one behind the other in a long line called a mule train.

Helicopters also come to our village. They carry people, but they can only fly when it is not windy.

Our food comes down on the mule train. The only thing the mule train cannot bring is ice-cream! The helicopter brings the ice-cream because it takes nearly a day for the mule train to get to our village from the top of the canyon.

If you post a letter from our village, it is marked with a special postmark to show it was delivered by mule train.

I got a bike for my birthday. It came on the mule train. One wheel was on the first mule, and the other wheel and the bike frame were on the next two mules. Mum helped me to put it together!

Chapter 3

My island home

I'm Ari and I live on a small island in the middle of the ocean. It is about halfway between South America and South Africa.

There is no airport on our island and it takes seven days on a boat to get to the nearest city.

This island,
Tristan da Cunha,
is the most isolated
settlement in the world.

About 300 people live on our island. We grow most of our food because we are so far from the shops.

There is not a lot of land for grazing, so each family can only have seven sheep and two cows. We also have ducks and chickens.

Every family has their own vegetable patch. We eat a lot of fish, too. My dad and I love to catch fish and lobsters. I love lobster pie with mashed potato on top.

There is one shop on the island. It sells all the other things we cannot grow ourselves.

If we want something we cannot get at the shop, we order it. Then we have to wait for it to be delivered by ship.

I had to wait weeks and weeks for my new fishing rod.

Chapter 4:
My lighthouse home

My name is Amy and I live on an island.
My dad is a park ranger. He also helps
to look after the lighthouse
next to our house.

Moreton Island
is off the coast
of Queensland,
Australia.

A long time ago, a lighthouse keeper had to light the lamp in the lighthouse every night to warn the ships. But now the light comes on automatically. If the light does not come on, my dad fixes it.

Last week, my mum was very sick. Usually in an emergency, the helicopter would take her to the doctor, but it was too windy.

We had to drive on the beach to get to the ferry to take us to the closest town.

We reached the ferry just in time.
We drove onto the ferry and it took us
to the mainland. It took us nearly all day
to get to the doctor.

I love living at the lighthouse, but sometimes
I wish we lived in a town so we could drive
to the doctor in five minutes.

But then I think about the families who used to live at the lighthouse long ago. When someone was sick, they had to wait for a ship to come. Sometimes, they had to wait weeks if the weather was bad.

When we need help in an emergency, we can get in the car and drive.

Conclusion

Gus

I like living so far away from school and only having lessons for a short time each day. I have a lot of freedom, and I love to help out on the busy cattle station.

Carla

I love living in our village because it is very quiet and peaceful. I like watching the mules come into the village with all the supplies. It's exciting when you have ordered something special.

Ari

I like living on an island in the middle of the ocean. Everyone who lives on the island helps each other. Growing our own food and fishing are really healthy ways to eat, and we definitely know where the food comes from!

Amy

I feel very special living at the lighthouse – I love watching the light shining across the sea at night. We have so many beautiful places to explore next to our home, and I get to go to the beach every day.

A note from the author

I enjoyed researching and writing this book. It was fascinating to learn about children who live so differently from most of us. These children are used to living far away from towns and cities. For them it is normal, and for some it would be strange to live any other way.

I was particularly interested to learn about children who used to live in lighthouses on islands. Often when their families left the lighthouses and moved to towns to live, the children had difficulty adjusting. They longed for the day when they could return and live in a home faraway from the rest of the world.